The Little Apple Tree

By Nia Peeples

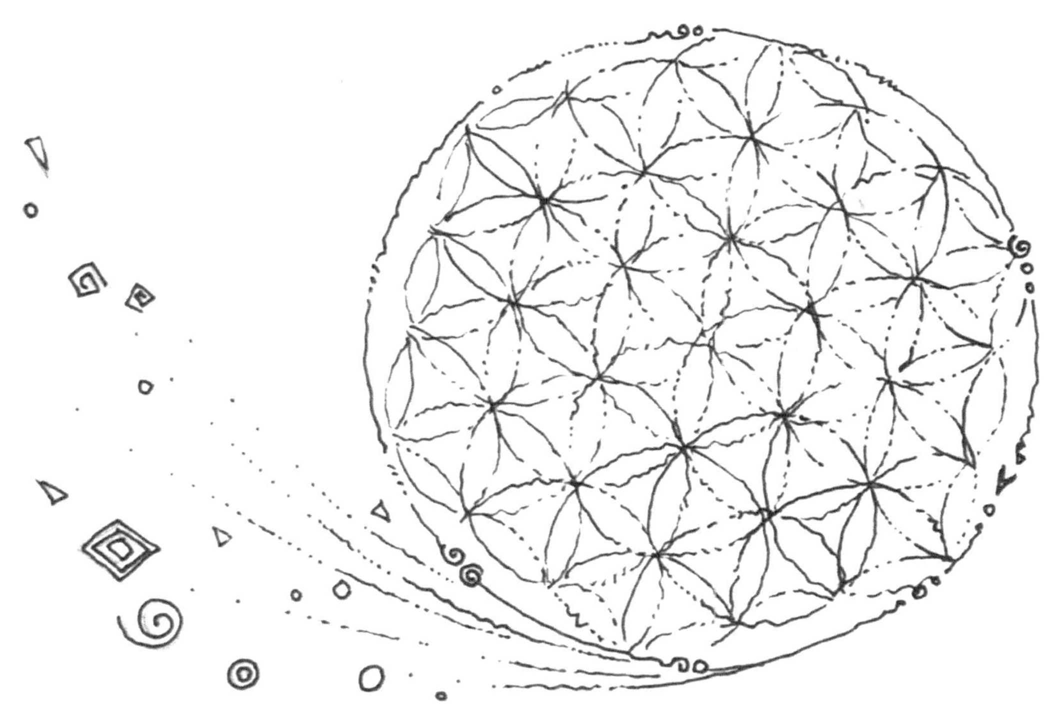

The Little Apple Tree, written By Nia Peeples
publisher: Seed Of Light Publications
book design and editing by Visual Art

ISBN: 978-0-9990540-0-0

Printed in the United States of America

First Edition

For Christopher and Sienna, the loves
of my life. And for all the children who
are, ever have been, and continue to be.

Your Dreams are Real.
Believe what you Feel.

Once there was a little tree. She was an
Apple Tree who lived happily in a little box,
in a little store.

One day a young man who dreamed
of being a farmer, fell in love with The Little
Apple Tree. He loved her so much that he
bought her and decided to start an apple farm.

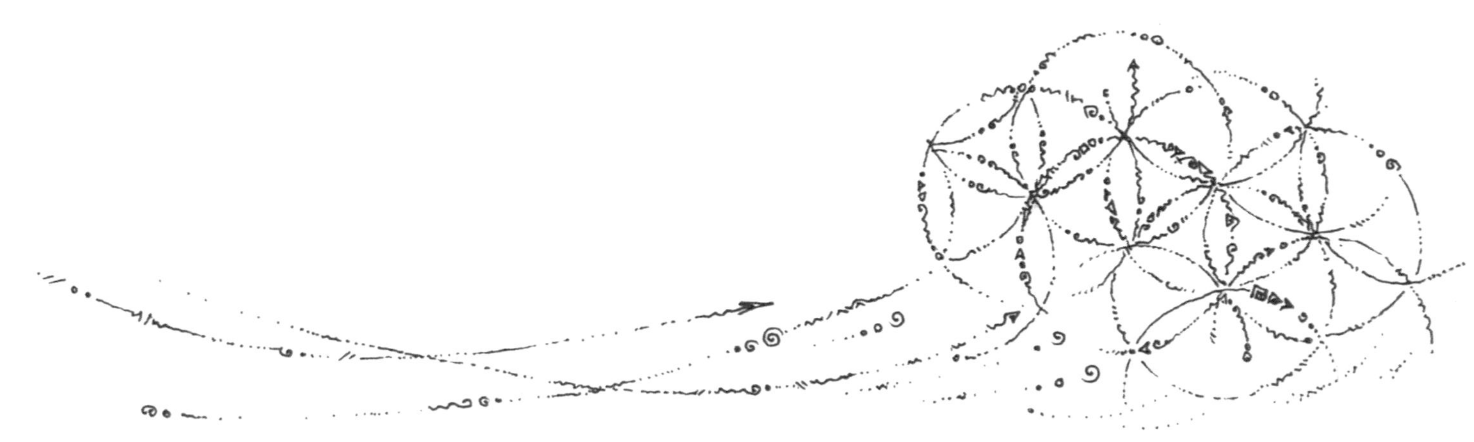

He promised to keep her safe and sound and give her everything she ever dreamed of. The Little Apple Tree loved him for that and promised to give him the best apples she could possibly make.

The Young Farmer loved The Little Apple Tree.

And she loved him.

And they both were very happy.

So The Young Farmer brought her home and lovingly placed The Little Apple Tree in her little box, in his little barn, beside his little house, to keep her out of the rain and sun and soil, so she could stay warm and dry.

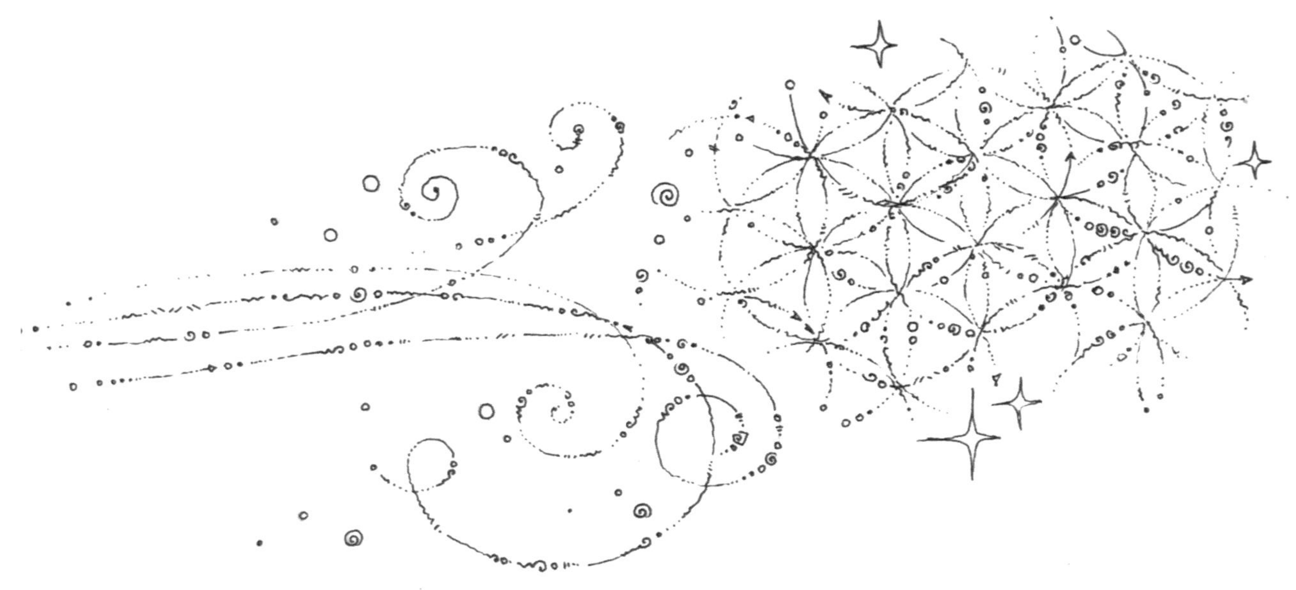

Every day, The Young Farmer would come to The Little Apple Tree to give her water and patiently wait for apples.

Finally one day, the Little Apple Tree surprised The Young Farmer with a beautiful red apple, sweet and delicious.

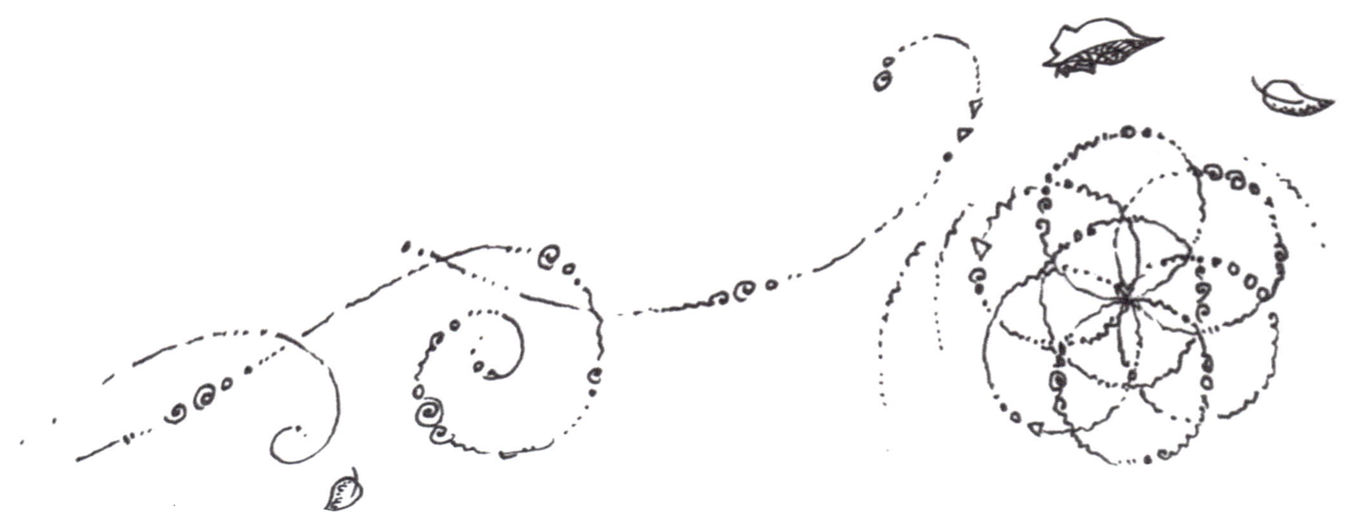

The Young Farmer loved The Little Apple Tree.

And she loved him.

And they both were very happy.

As time went on, The Little Apple Tree began to grow. She grew and grew and grew until before long, her head was up to the ceiling and her roots were popping out of her little box.

W anting to keep her safe, The Young
Farmer trimmed her roots so they would fit
into the box. And he cut her branches so her
head wouldn't hit the ceiling.

As she stood up straight and tall,
The Little Apple Tree thanked him for this and
promised to stay small and give him even more
of the best apples she could possibly make.

But The Little Apple Tree continued
to grow, and grow and grow. She tried her
hardest to stay small and make lots of apples
for the Young Farmer. But there, in her little
box, in his little barn, she just couldn't stay
small enough or make any more apples.

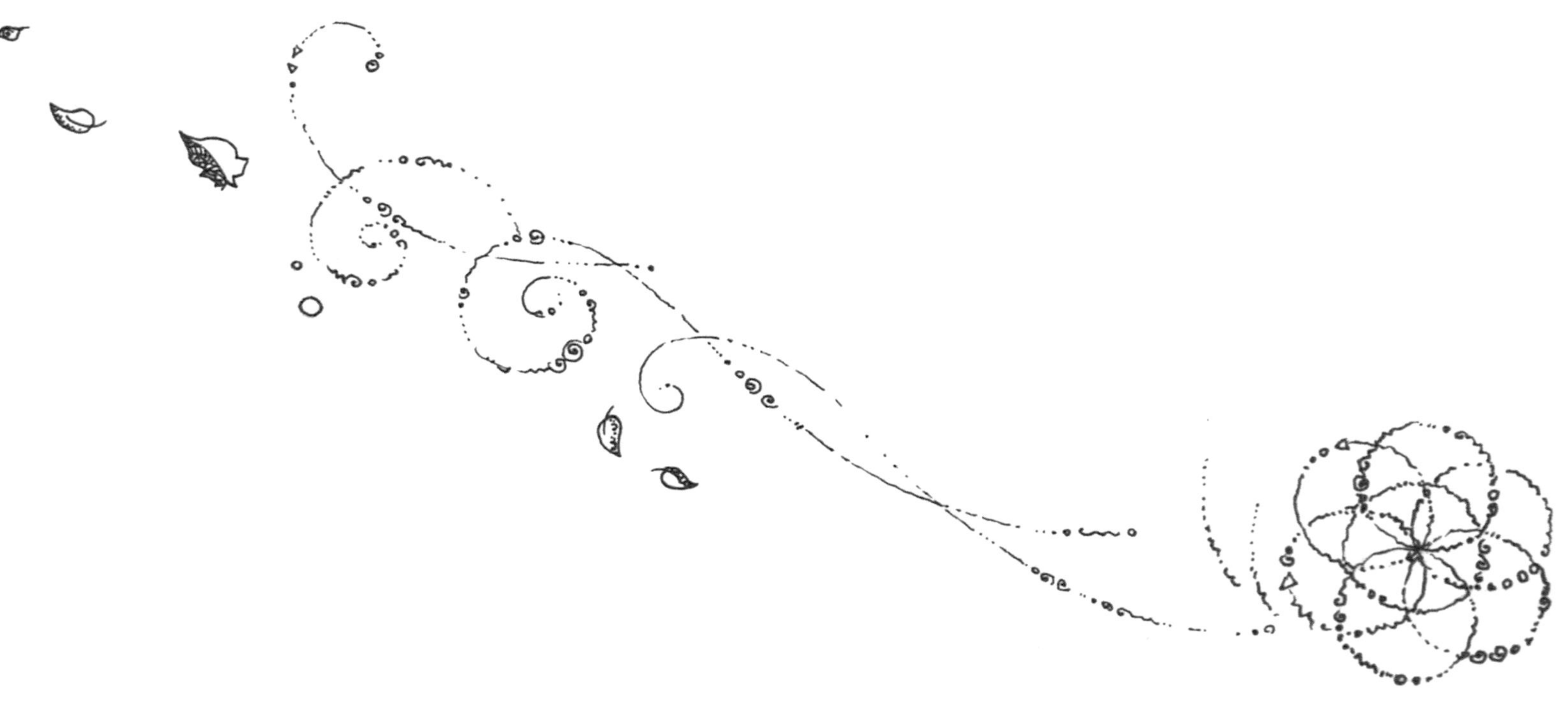

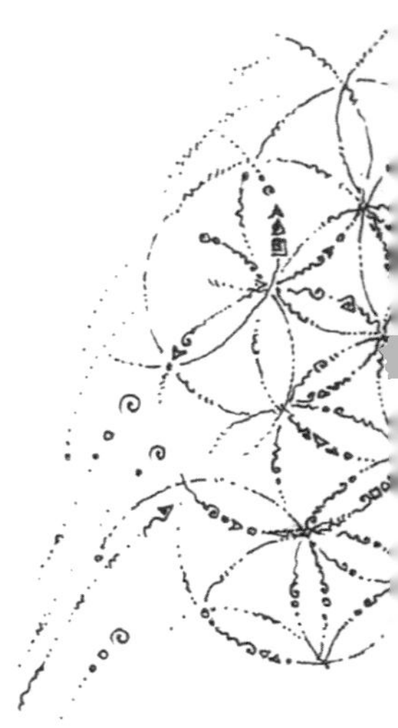

And the young farmer would come
every day to trim and cut and saw. He tried his
hardest to keep her safe in her little box, in his
little barn out of the rain and sun and soil but
it was a lot of work. And he was getting very
tired.

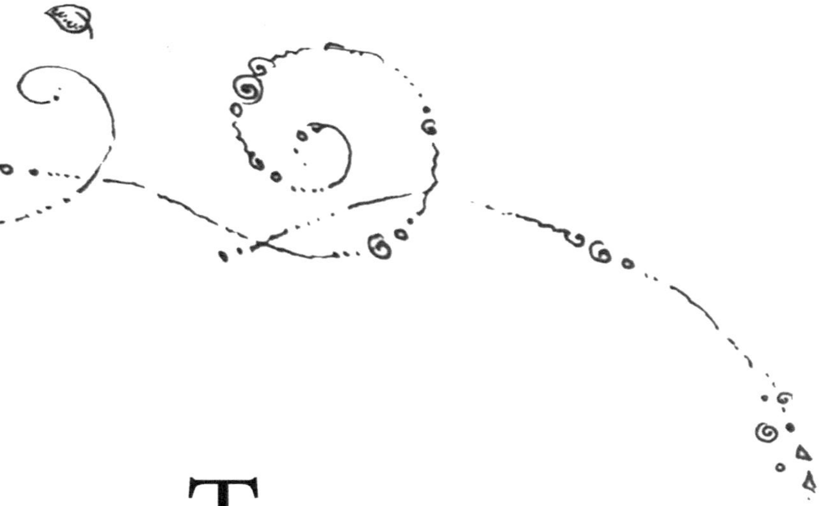

The Young Farmer loved The Little Apple Tree

And she loved him.

But now, neither of them was very happy.

Then one night as The Little Apple Tree
slept, she had a dream that she was no longer
a little apple tree, but a gigantic, full, proud
apple tree as tall as the clouds were high, with
hundreds of beautiful red apples, so many
apples that no one could even count them.

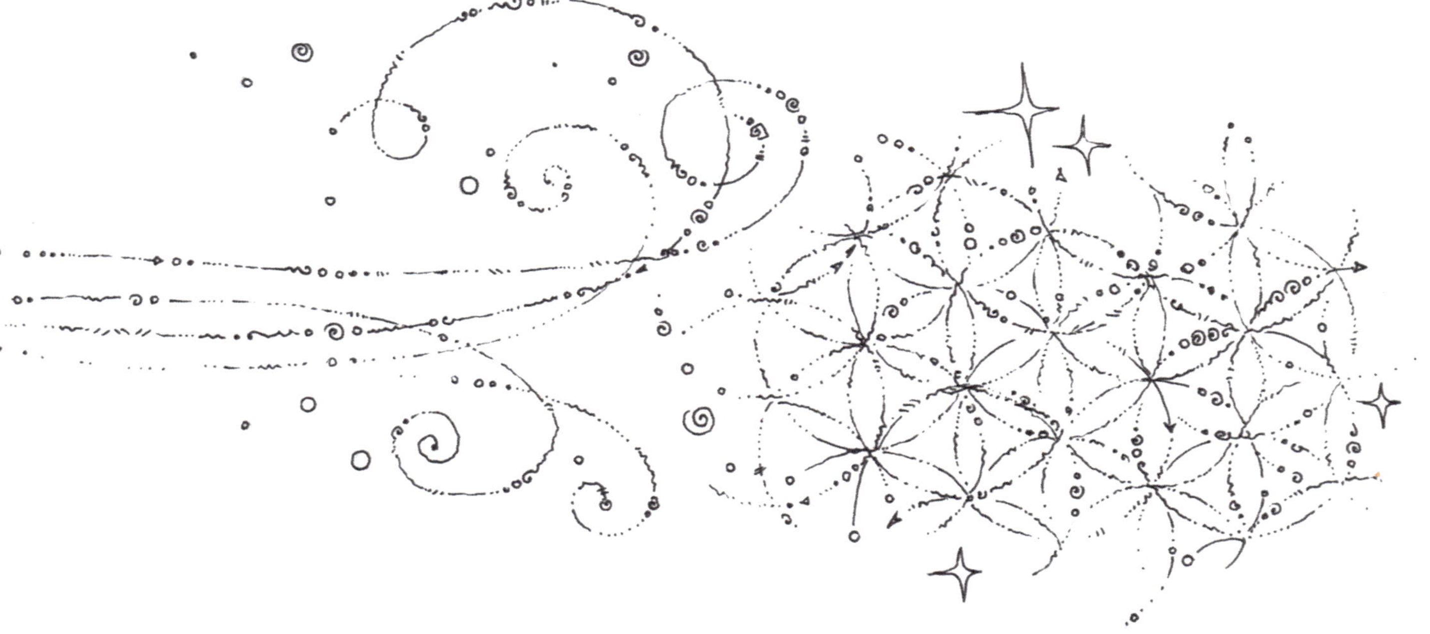

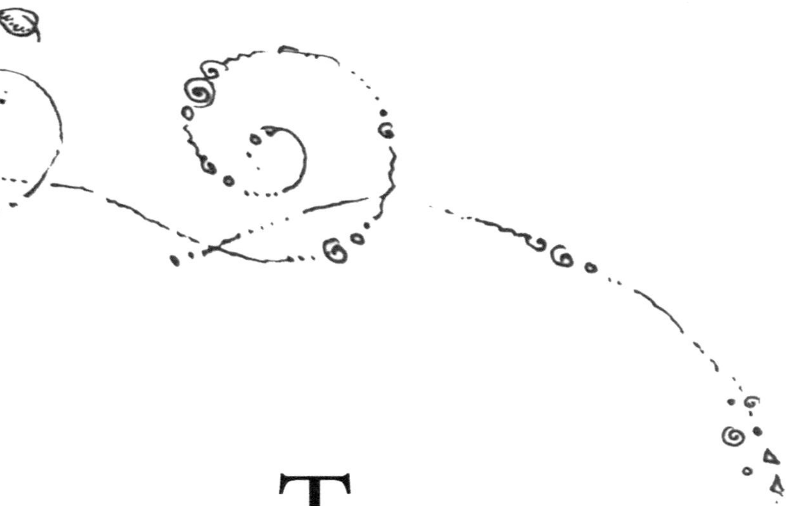

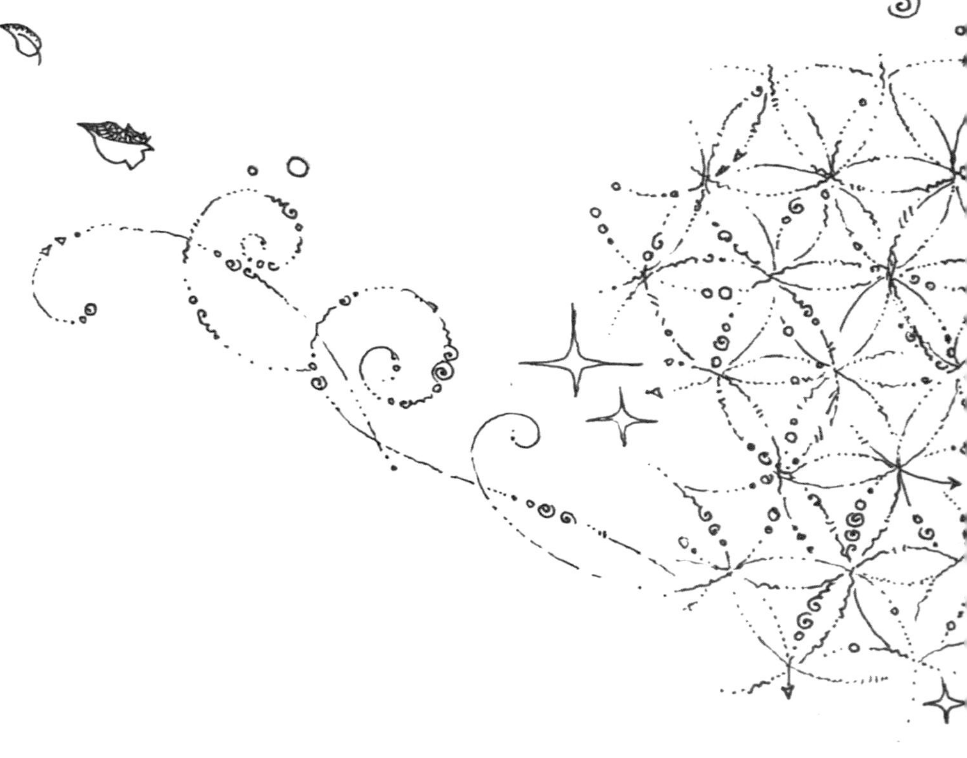

The next morning as The Little Apple
Tree awakened, she remembered her dream
and felt so very happy, happier than she'd ever
felt. And as she held on to that warm happy
feeling, something wonderful, yet a little
frightening happened.

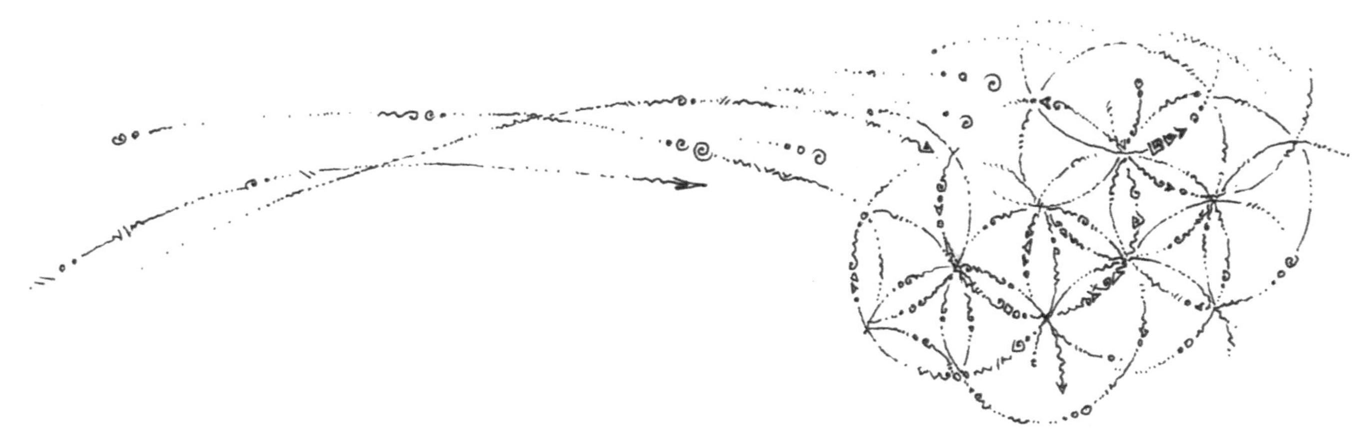

She began to grow and grow and grow more than ever before. She grew so much that her roots snapped apart her little box, and broke through the floor, digging deep into the rich moist soil beneath.

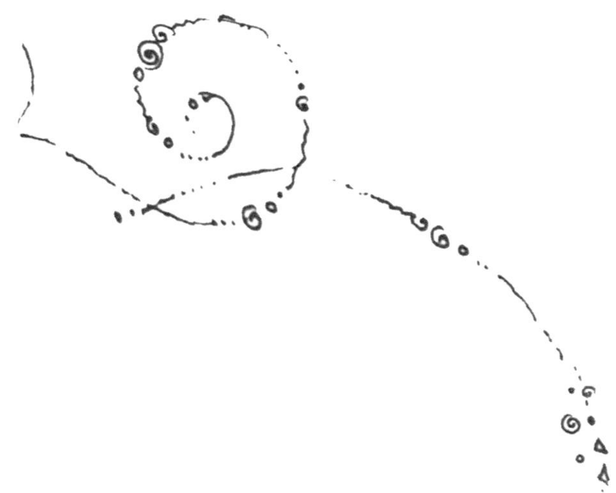

Her head crashed through the ceiling and up into the sky toward the morning clouds as hundreds of bright red apples burst froth from her branches!

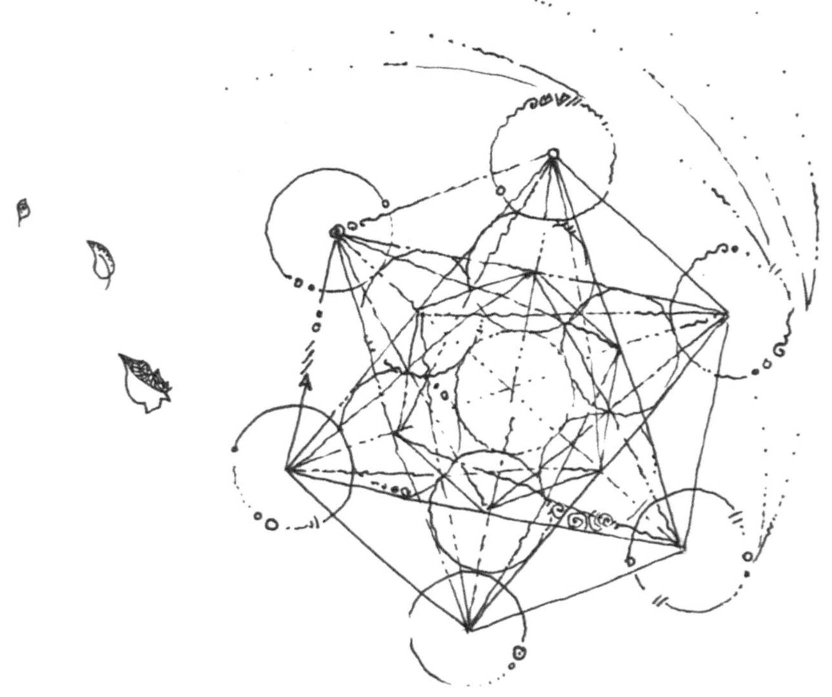

She gasped with delight for she knew she
had become The Magnificent Apple Tree she
was always meant to be. She was so happy that
she laughed and laughed out loud with joy!

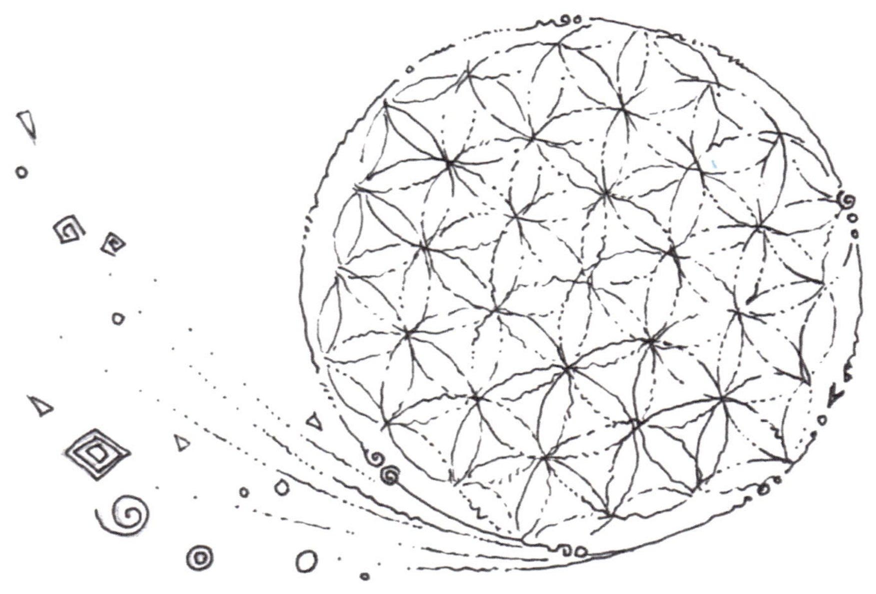

... until she looked down and saw the
Young Farmer crying as he sat on one of the
many broken pieces of his little barn.

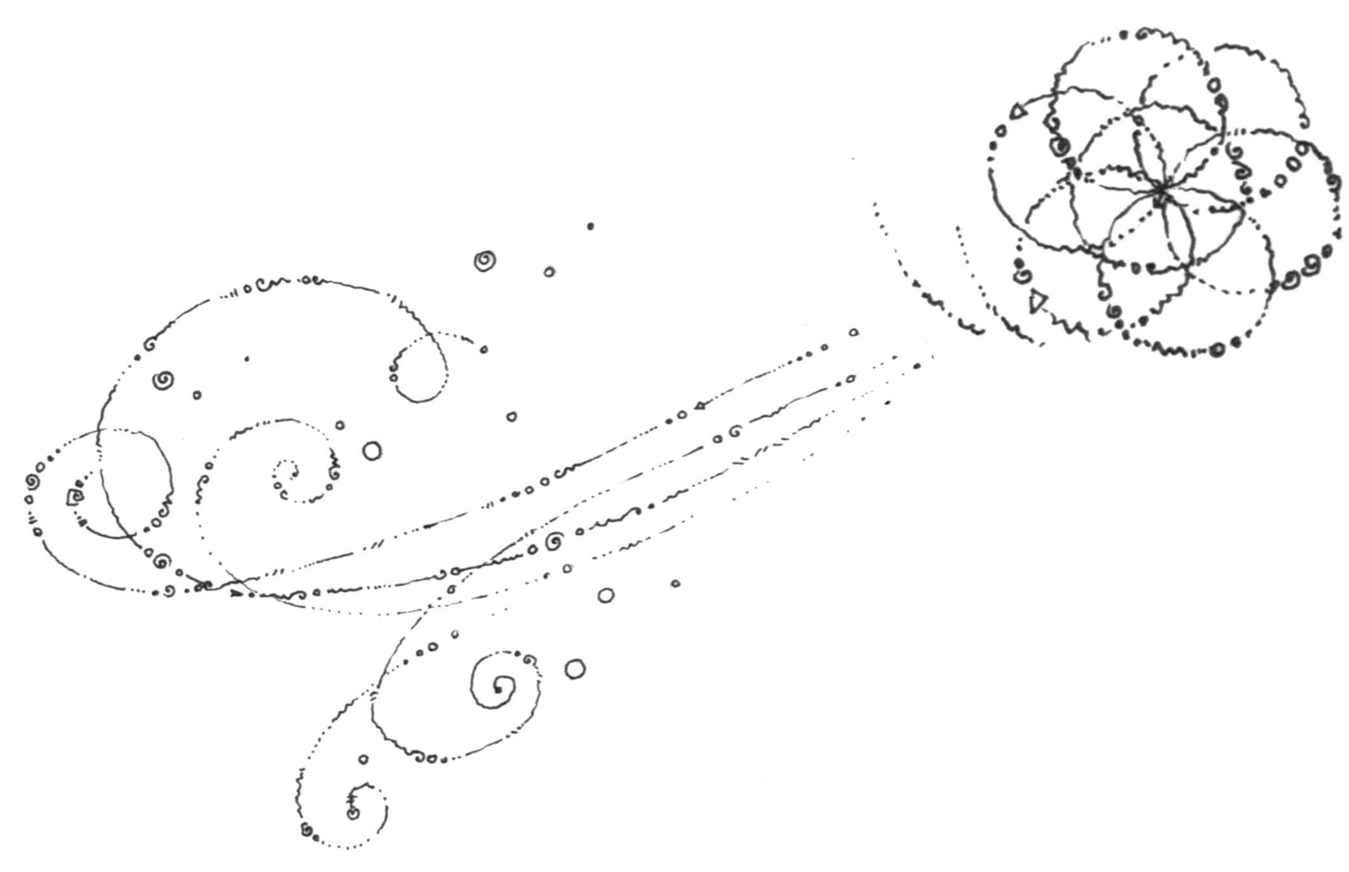

The Young Farmer looked up at
The Magnificent Apple Tree and cried,
"What have I done? Did I not love you
enough? I trimmed and cut and watered you
every day to keep you safe. Why have you torn
down my little barn and grown so tall I can
not take care of you any more?"

At first, The Magnificent Apple Tree felt bad. Then she explained to The Young Farmer that she loved him for taking care of her but an Apple tree cannot live inside a barn. An Apple Tree needs the rain and the sun and the soil to become all it was meant to be.

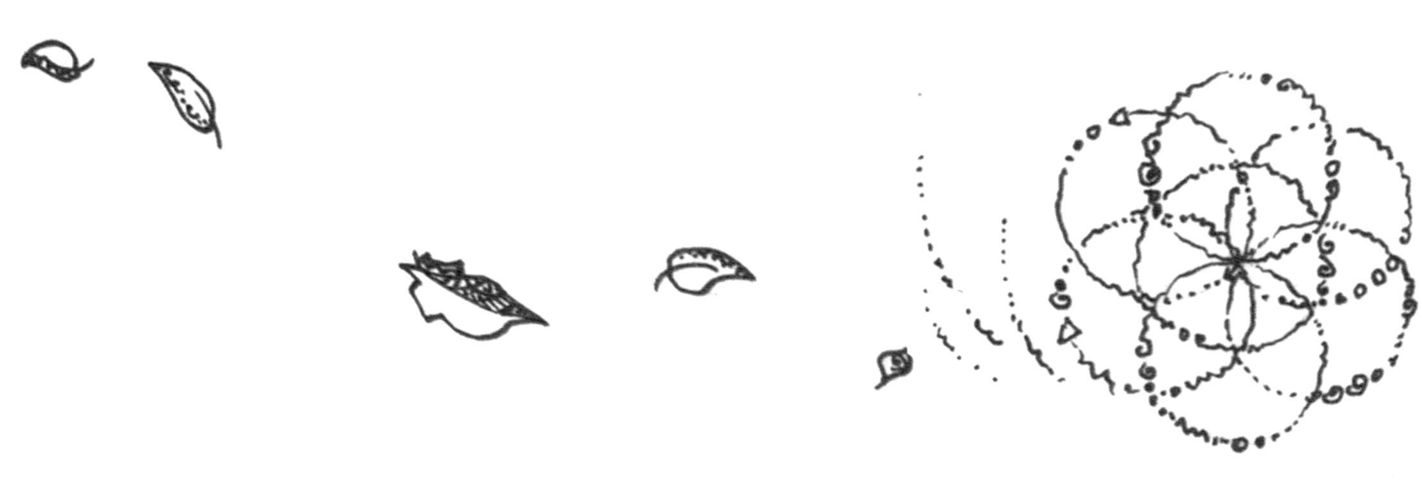

But The Young Farmer was so hurt and unhappy that he stormed back to his little house and cried and cried and cried.

Then that night, as The Young Farmer slept, he dreamed that his Magnificent Apple Tree, outside in the rain and sun and soil, became many little apple trees. And those little apple trees became many more Magnificent Apple Trees and soon he had an apple farm with apples as far as the eye could see.

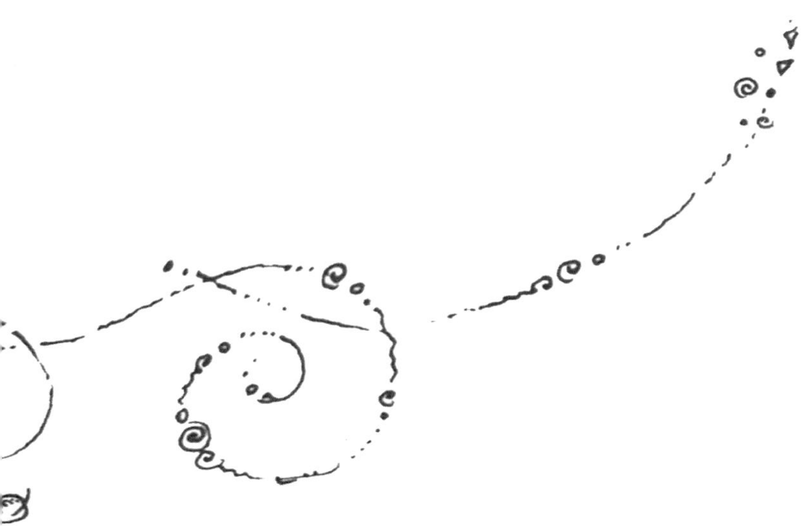

The next morning as The Young Farmer
awakened, he remembered his dream and
felt so very happy, happier than he'd ever felt.
And as he held on to that warm happy feeling,
something wonderful, yet a little frightening
happened.

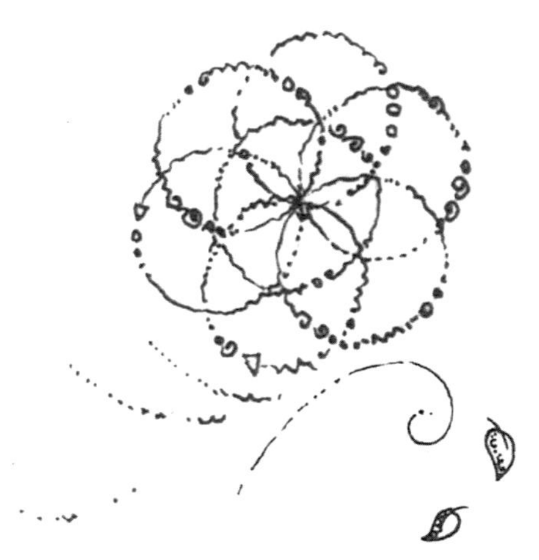

He marched outside and began to tear down the rest of his little barn and plow the field to make space for more apple trees to be planted.

It was hard work, harder than trimming and cutting and sawing to keep the Little Apple Tree inside her little box inside the little barn.

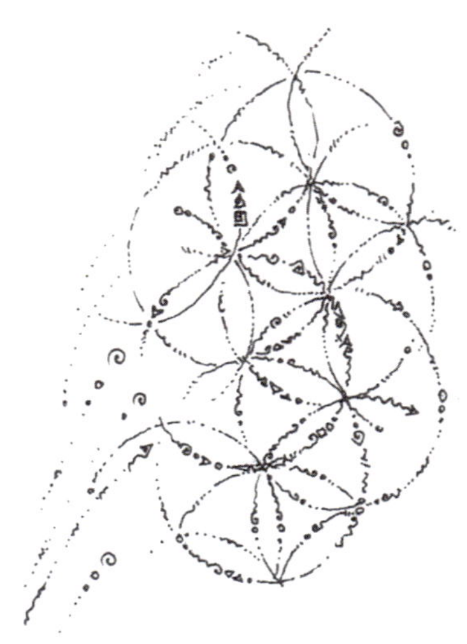

But he gasped with delight for he knew he could become The Magnificent Farmer he was always meant to be.

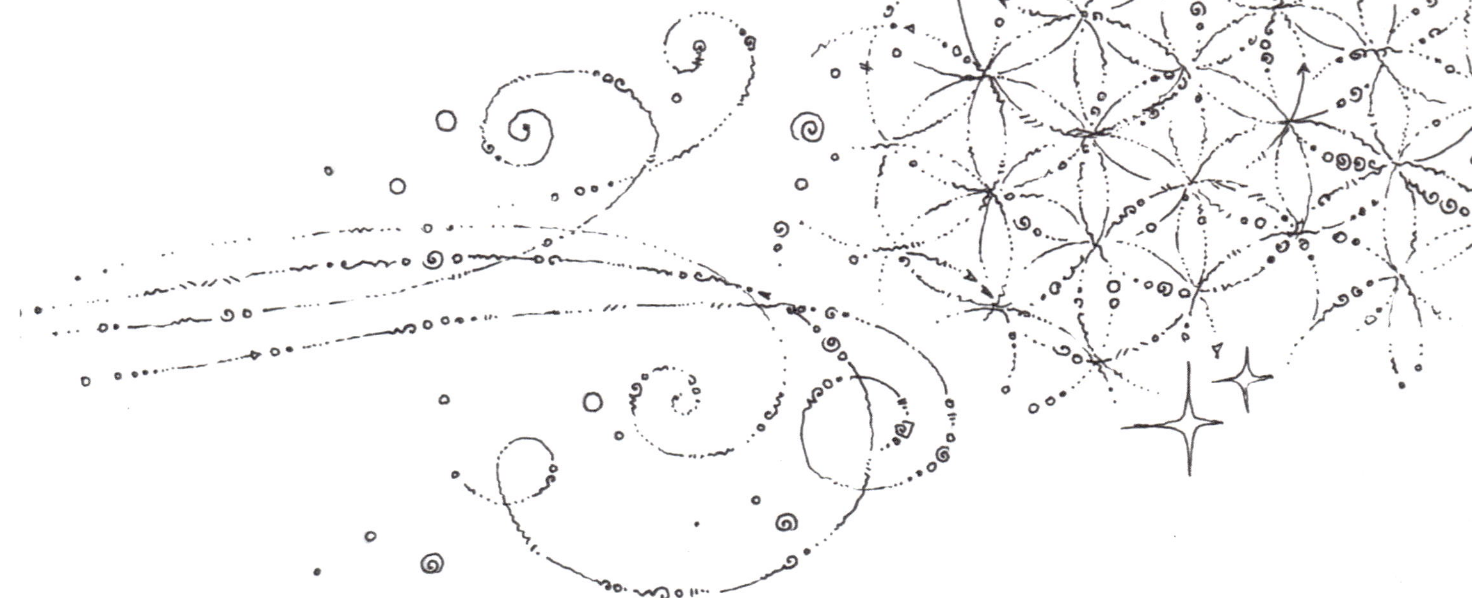

And as he worked, he laughed out loud with joy and looked up at The Magnificent Apple Tree and shouted, "Thank you! Thank you for being the Magnificent Apple Tree you were always meant to be for you have taught me how to become the Magnificent Farmer I was always meant to be."

The Magnificent Farmer loved

The Magnificent Apple Tree

And she loved him.

And they both were very, *very* happy.

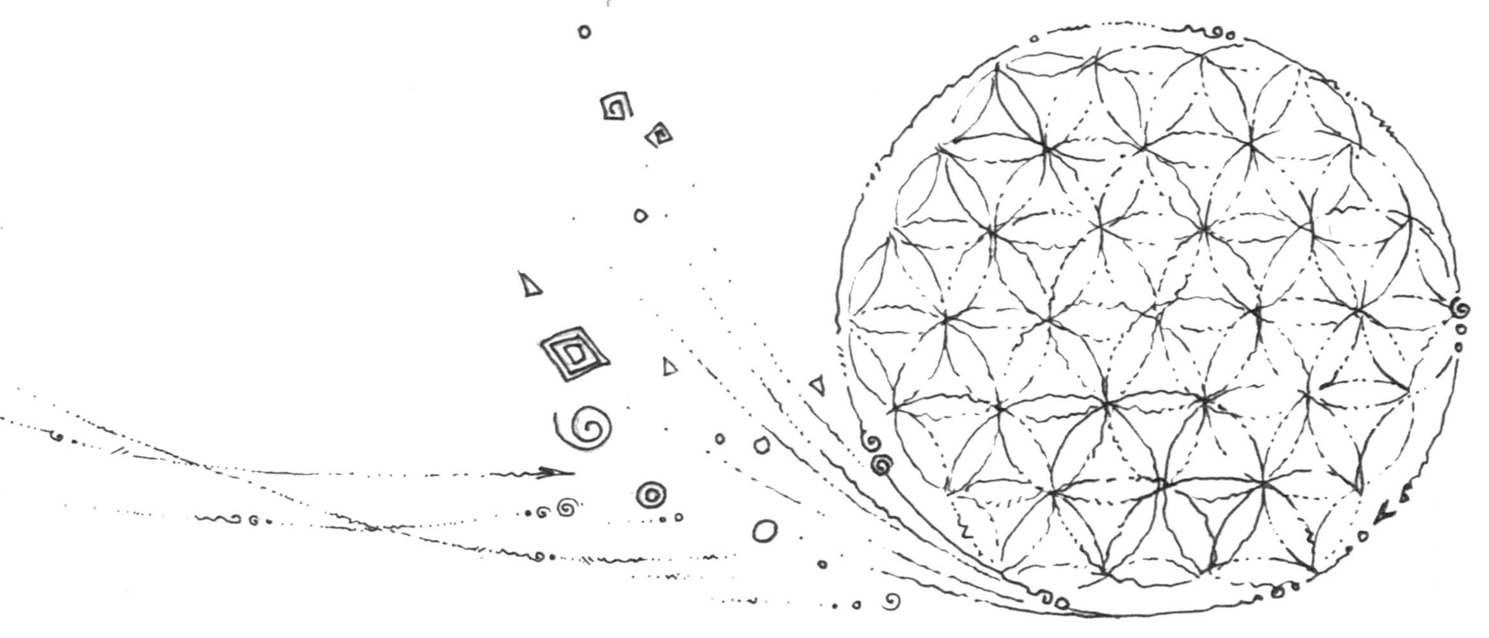

Made in the USA
Monee, IL
16 August 2023